What does it mean to be
British?

Nick Hunter

a Capstone company — publishers for children

Raintree is an imprint of Capstone Global Library Limited, a company incorporated in England and Wales having its registered office at 264 Banbury Road, Oxford, OX2 7DY – Registered company number: 6695582

www.raintree.co.uk
myorders@raintree.co.uk

Text © Capstone Global Library Limited 2017
The moral rights of the proprietor have been asserted.

Edited by Linda Staniford
Designed by Steve Mead
Picture research by Tracy Cummins
Originated by Capstone Global Library Ltd
Produced by Victoria Fitzgerald
Printed and bound in China

ISBN 978 1 4747 4059 3
20 19 18 17 16
10 9 8 7 6 5 4 3 2 1

British Library Cataloguing in Publication Data
A full catalogue record for this book is available from the Bri

Acknowledgements
We would like to thank the following for permission to reprc

Getty Images: ANDY BUCHANAN, 24, David Ramos, 22, Gary Wolstenholme, 4, Matthew Horwood, 28, Mr Puttnam/ IWM, 9 Top, OLI SCARFF/AFP, 23, Ray Collins - WPA Pool, 13 Bottom, Rob Stothard, 16, VisitBritain/Andrew Pickett, 19; Newscom: Ben Cawthra/Sipa USA, 20; Shutterstock: Asianet-Pakistan, 25, BasPhoto, 26, Bikeworldtravel, 27, Brian Maudsley, 17, Clive Chilvers, 18, DeiMosz, Design Element, Everett - Art, 11, Everett Historical, 8, james weston, Design Element, jason cox, 5 Bottom, John Gomez, 15, jorisvo, 21, Julia Remezova, 29, Katariina Järvinen, 10, Lucky Luke, 7, MarcAndreLeTourneux, 5 Top, mattasbestos, 31, Qing Ding, 6, r.nagy, 13 Top, Rawpixel.com, Cover, 1, Sergey Mastepanov, Design Element, Sideways Design, 9 Bottom; Thinkstock: Photos.com, 14

We would like to thank Marguerite Heath, Programmes Director at the Citizenship Foundation, for her invaluable help in the preparation of this book.

Disclaimer
All the internet addresses (URLs) given in this book were valid at the time of going to press. However, due to the dynamic nature of the internet, some addresses may have changed, or sites may have changed or ceased to exist since publication. While the author and publishers regret any inconvenience this may cause readers, no responsibility for any such changes can be accepted by either the author or the publishers.

Contents

Who are the British?

If someone asks you where you live, what do you say? There are lots of possible answers to that question. Do they mean your house number and street name, or which city or town you live in? You could be from Aberystwyth, Belfast, Colchester or Dundee. If you're talking to someone from another country, you might just say, "I'm from Britain, also called the United Kingdom".

These people came from all over the British Isles to watch the 2012 London Olympics.

STATS

How many British people are there?

The United Kingdom is home to more than 65 million people. Most of those people are British citizens but around 5 million are citizens of other countries. There are also nearly 5 million British citizens living outside the UK.

Britain or the UK's full name is the United Kingdom of Great Britain and Northern Ireland. It is made up of England, Scotland, Wales and Northern Ireland. It lies on the northwestern edge of Europe. It includes the island of Great Britain, part of the island of Ireland and hundreds of other islands, such as the Orkney and Shetland Islands to the north of Scotland.

Some British people live in tiny communities like this one in the Shetland Islands.

British citizens need a passport to visit other countries and return home.

Who are the British people?

The **citizens** of the UK are called the British people. If you were born in the UK, you are a British citizen. Many citizens move to the UK from other countries, and choose to become British citizens. Many British people choose to live in other countries around the world.

This book will look at the things these people have in common and try to discover what it means to be British.

What are the different parts of the United Kingdom?

The United Kingdom's name comes from the way the country developed throughout history, with separate kingdoms joining to form one country. The UK is made up of four separate **nations.**

England is both the biggest and most crowded nation of the United Kingdom. England is home to the UK's vast capital city, London, which attracts people from around the world to live and work. People in different regions of England, such as Yorkshire or Cornwall, are proud of the things that make them different. These things might be the special words they use or the sports teams they support.

The landscape of Britain ranges from bustling cities to dramatic coasts, like this one in County Antrim, Northern Ireland.

Scotland and England have shared the same king or queen since 1603. In 1707, Scotland's leaders agreed to join the **governments** of England and Scotland in an agreement called the Act of Union. Not all Scots were happy about this and many Scots today believe that Scotland should be an **independent** country, and no longer part of the UK.

STATS

National names
The most popular baby names are different depending where you are born in the UK. In 2012, English babies were most likely to be called Harry or Amelia, while there were more Sophies and Jacks born in Scotland and Northern Ireland.

Wales is called Cymru in the Welsh language. English **monarchs** had tried to rule Wales for hundreds of years, before King Henry VIII passed a law in 1536 to join the two countries together officially.

Northern Ireland has existed since 1921, when the rest of the island of Ireland left the United Kingdom to become an independent country.

The different countries and regions of the UK sometimes disagree with each other, but they share many things. Each country chooses its government. The **Head of State**, or chief representative of the country, is the Queen or King.

SYMBOLS OF BRITAIN

The Union Jack
The Union Jack is the flag of the United Kingdom. It was first used in 1606, shortly after King James VI of Scotland became King of England and Wales too. The flag combines the flags of England, Scotland and Northern Ireland.

Do British people have a shared history?

The United Kingdom and the British people have been shaped by their history. In the past, Britain's people have defeated attempts to invade the country. The UK's contact with other parts of the world has also brought people to Britain whose ancestors were not British.

From the 1500s, British explorers and traders founded settlements in distant lands from Africa to India. These areas were ruled by the British and became the **British Empire**. The British Empire brought great riches to the UK and its traders, but was not good for all its people. The settlers brought diseases and often treated people badly.

Millions of Africans were captured as slaves and taken from their homes by British slave traders.

Between 1939 and 1945, British people worked together to defeat Nazi Germany when its forces invaded most of Europe. Prime Minister Winston Churchill said this was the British people's "finest hour".

More recently, many people from the Caribbean, India, Pakistan and other areas that were once part of the British Empire have moved to Britain. They have become British citizens, even though they do not share many parts of British history.

SYMBOLS OF BRITAIN

The National Anthem

Do you know the words to "God Save the Queen"? It's the British national anthem, or song. You often hear it played before sporting events, or when a British athlete wins a gold medal at the Olympic Games. The oldest printed version of the song was made in 1745.

What languages do British people speak?

English is spoken by billions of people around the world. This language spread from the UK and 9 out of 10 British people speak English as their main language.

The English language itself has developed gradually as people from other parts of the world settled in the British Isles. It was based on the language of settlers from Germany more than 1000 years ago, and new words have been added from French and many other languages. Words are still being added all the time.

Road signs in Wales are printed in Welsh and English

English is not the only language spoken by British people. Welsh is the other official language in the UK, spoken in many areas of Wales. In parts of Scotland and Northern Ireland, people speak Scots and Gaelic languages. Families that have moved to the UK may continue to speak their home languages, among which are Urdu and Polish.

Should all British people speak English? Some people think so, but one of the most important **rights** British people enjoy is the right to freedom of expression, which means they can speak in whatever language they choose.

STATS

Will's words

William Shakespeare was the greatest writer in English. He died more than 400 years ago but his poems and plays are read and performed around the world. Shakespeare's writings included around 2000 words that had never been written down before and he was the first to use phrases such as "a heart of gold" or "in a pickle".

Who rules the United Kingdom?

The Queen or King is the Head of State, or leader of the country, but he or she does not make the rules. The government, chosen by the British people, decides which laws to pass. Every adult is able to have a say in what happens in the United Kingdom.

The United Kingdom is a **democracy**. Democracy means rule by the people. Every adult can vote in a **general election**. Each area of the UK elects a Member of **Parliament** (MP) from different political groups or parties. The party with the most MPs forms the government and its leader is the Prime Minister of the UK. In 2016, Theresa May of the Conservative Party became Prime Minister. Parliament votes on new laws planned by the government.

Scotland, Wales and Northern Ireland have separate governments, which are chosen by elections. Elections are also used to choose members of local councils. The councils make rules for cities and other local areas.

STATS

Does everyone live in a democracy?
Many people are unable to choose their government. Around half the countries in the world have some form of democracy. In one-third of the countries in the world people have no say in who rules them.

More than 600 Members of Parliament meet in Westminster, London.

The birth of democracy

The United Kingdom was one of the first countries in which the people chose the government. Before the 1900s only wealthier men were allowed to vote. It was not until 1928 that all adult men and women could vote in general elections.

SYMBOLS OF BRITAIN

The Monarch

Queen Elizabeth II became Queen of the United Kingdom in 1952. She is Head of State but she does not have the power to make laws.

What protections and rights do British people have?

Many countries have a written **constitution**. This document says what rights the citizens of that country have, and what the government is allowed to do. Rights are freedoms and protections that everyone has. For example, people in Britain have a right not to be imprisoned unless they commit a crime.

Britain does not have a single constitution. British people's rights are protected by lots of different rules and laws agreed over centuries of history. The first of these was Magna Carta, signed more than 800 years ago in 1215. King John was forced to sign Magna Carta. He agreed to respect the rights of his people and could no longer do whatever he wanted.

Magna Carta was one of the first agreements about the rights of a king and his people.

Obeying the law

The **Rule of Law** is an essential part of the United Kingdom's constitution. According to this idea, everyone is expected to obey the law, including the government, police and the army. This protects the rights of every citizen in the UK.

Courts and judges, also called the **judiciary**, decide whether any law has been broken. For this reason, the judiciary is always independent of the rest of the government.

British people have the right to disagree with the government. These people are protesting against plans to change doctors' working conditions.

CASE STUDY

Rights in the UK

Omar was forced to flee from his home in Syria by a terrible civil war. He risked his life to reach the UK and hopes that one day his family will be able to join him:

"I knew that [the UK] gave rights to people. I wanted to come here and work and start from zero".

source: Refugee Action

What religions do British people follow?

British people have the right to follow whatever religious beliefs they choose. People can also decide to have no religious beliefs. Christianity is the most common religion in Britain, but there are communities following all of the world's major religions.

These Musllims are celebrating the festival of Eid in Southwark, London.

STATS

Changing religion
For much of the UK's history, most British people were Christians. This is changing and researchers have predicted that fewer than half of all Britons will be Christians in 2050. Around 1 in 10 British people will be Muslims. The number of British people with no religion is also expected to increase.

As with many areas of British life, religious freedom is tied up with the country's history. The monarch is automatically head of the Church of England. He or she must always be a Protestant Christian, since England broke away from the Catholic Church in the 1500s. In modern Britain the monarch is also expected to represent other Christians, including members of the Catholic Church, and followers of other religions.

Tolerance and understanding of other religions is an important part of British life. Workplaces and schools are not allowed to treat people differently because of their religious beliefs.

Fighting intolerance

Understanding other people's beliefs is not always easy. Some religious followers believe that those who follow other religions are wrong. Sometimes, opposition to other religions can lead to violence. In the United Kingdom, leaders of all major religious groups speak out against violence.

Around the UK, you can see signs that religious communities did not always live together peacefully. King Henry VIII destroyed many Catholic churches and religious buildings such as Whitby Abbey in the 1500s.

What is British culture?

Your religion may be one aspect of your culture. Culture is the word that describes the different elements of a person's or group's lifestyle. It can include your language, religion, clothes, music and many other aspects of the way you live.

Just as there is no single British language or religion, there is really no single British culture. If you travelled from one end of Britain to the other, through **rural** counties and cities like Birmingham and Glasgow, you would come across a dizzying variety of festivals, music, and even food that are all part of British culture. British culture is open to new ideas and influences.

London's Notting Hill Carnival was started by the Caribbean community in 1964. It has become Europe's largest street festival.

People from different cultures who live in Britain, or who have moved there from other countries, have shaped the huge variations in British culture. This has happened over centuries. When Norman invaders came from France in 1066, they brought food flavoured with spices from Asia. More recently, communities from Asian countries such as China have brought new dishes of rice and noodles. They combine sweet and savoury flavours, changing them to suit British tastes.

Find out more

Local culture

British culture is different wherever you live in the United Kingdom. Your local culture will be shaped by the history of the area and the people who have moved there. See what you can discover about music and dance, art and craft, special foods, holidays and celebrations, and any particular local traditions.

Scottish Highland dancing is a traditional style of dancing performed to bagpipe music.

What are Britain's links with Europe and the world?

The United Kingdom is not a big country. Russia, the world's largest country, is 70 times bigger. For every person living in the UK there are 23 people in China. But the UK has a strong voice in the world through many international organizations.

All countries in the world are members of the **United Nations (UN)**. The UK also has a permanent place on the United Nations Security Council, which tries to keep peace between countries. British armed forces are often involved in UN peacekeeping forces, sent to end or prevent wars around the world.

British people send money and supplies to help some of the world's poorest people, and the UK is home to aid organizations such as Oxfam.

The European Union

Since 1973, the UK has been a member of the **European Union** (EU). This has enabled the UK to trade with Europe. British people can live and work freely in other European countries.

Many British people felt that the EU had too much influence over the United Kingdom. In 2016, a **majority** of British people voted to leave the EU, although most people in Scotland and Northern Ireland voted to remain. New agreements with the other countries of Europe will change many areas of British life.

CASE STUDY

Leaving the EU

"It's a bit shocking, it's put a lot of uncertainty into Scotland over the next couple of years. This has split us right down the middle." Caroline, Aberdeen, Scotland

"I voted to leave. My principal reason was one of sovereignty, governance, or determining our own governance." Duncan, British person living in France.

(Source: Reuters)

How is Britain's population changing?

The British population has always been made up of people who have moved from other countries. In the past, these have included Romans from the south, and Anglo-Saxons and Vikings from northern Europe. French-speaking Normans were the last people to invade England in 1066, but people have continued to move, or migrate to the UK. People who move from one country to another are called **immigrants**.

Since 2000, many immigrants have come to the UK from elsewhere in the European Union. By 2014, more than 1 person in 10 in the UK was born in another country. The highest numbers of recent immigrants come from India, Poland and Pakistan.

Over 760,000 British people have chosen to settle in Spain.

STATS

Britons abroad
We often hear about immigrants settling in the UK, but millions of British-born people also live overseas. More than 1 million Britons live in Australia. The other top countries for immigrants from Britain are the USA, Canada, Ireland and Spain.

For and against immigration

Immigration has brought many benefits to the UK. People who move to the UK often do important jobs, such as working as doctors or nurses. Just by coming to Britain and using shops, restaurants and schools they make jobs for other people. As we have seen, immigration helps to create a varied culture.

However, some people claim that immigrants take jobs that British people could do. Opponents of immigration also believe large groups of people who do not share Britain's traditional language and culture can change communities too quickly.

Many immigrants work in hospitals and other essential services.

What are British values?

It is not easy to say what it means to be British. The people of the UK speak different languages. They follow different religions. Some British people may not even feel very British, such as the many Scots who voted for Scotland to leave the United Kingdom in 2014.

Values are ideas or principles that we think are important. Individuals can have their own values but there are some values that apply across the United Kingdom and unite British people.

British values are rights that British people have, but everyone also has responsibilities as part of those values.

Scottish people in Glasgow show their support for Scottish independence from the UK.

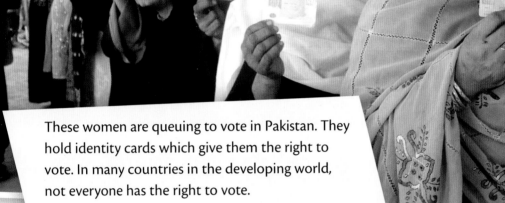

These women are queuing to vote in Pakistan. They hold identity cards which give them the right to vote. In many countries in the developing world, not everyone has the right to vote.

Democracy

Adult British citizens have the right to vote in elections to decide who will represent them in Parliament and on other bodies such as the local council. With that right comes a responsibility to use our vote wisely and to learn about the issues and people we vote for. Democracy rarely produces a result that everyone is happy with, but voters also have a responsibility to accept the result of an election.

STATS

The right to vote
At the UK General Election in 2015, 46.4 million people were registered to vote but more than a third did not cast a vote. In some countries, such as Australia, voting is compulsory, but adults can choose whether to vote in the UK.

The Rule of Law

The law of the United Kingdom protects people's rights in many ways. The government and the police have to obey the law as well as enforce it. In return for these rights, British citizens are expected to know what is right and wrong according to our values and to follow the law.

Liberty

British people expect to have the liberty or freedom to do whatever they want without breaking the law. In order for this to work, we have a responsibility to ensure that our actions will not harm others and will generally be good for society.

The Old Bailey Criminal Court in London has this statue on the top. It represents Justice, holding a sword and scales.

Respect and tolerance

In a **diverse** country such as the modern United Kingdom, it is important to recognize that people have different views. We may not all share a religion, or political views, but we accept that people have a right to hold their views.

We all have a right to expect tolerance and respect for our views. We also have a responsibility to give others that same tolerance and respect.

"Humour has to come high on the list. ... Banter, self-mockery and laughing at ill-luck surely do constitute one of our strongest ... qualities. "

Writer Stephen Fry gives his own thoughts on British values.

The British sense of humour: a runner in the London Marathon wears fancy dress.

What makes you British?

Being British means different things to different people. Some Britons are proud of the country's history and traditions such as the Royal Family; others celebrate the diversity of Britain's cities. What values do you think are important?

Many of us will have several identities. You may feel English, Scottish, Welsh, Indian or Jamaican as well as British. You may celebrate different religious festivals from some of your friends. Having more than one identity won't affect your British values such as belief in democracy or tolerance.

These football fans feel Welsh as well as British.

SYMBOLS OF BRITAIN

National symbols

The bulldog has traditionally been a symbol of the British people. It represents having a stubborn character and never giving in. What is the one thing that symbolizes Britain for you? It could be an animal like the bulldog, a person or almost anything that you think sums up British values.

Remember that British values are not fixed. Britain is a democracy now, but a century ago most women could not vote in elections. The UK population is constantly changing, so values like religious tolerance have become more important. You and your generation will have the opportunity to shape the values that you think are important for the future.

Try it yourself

School democracy

Democracy can work in schools too. Many schools explore democracy by holding elections of their own. Does your school hold elections for a school council or something similar? If not, you could ask your teachers about holding an election.

Glossary

British Empire collection of different countries and colonies ruled by Britain, which included many parts of the world in 1900

citizen someone who is officially a member of a state or country

constitution the agreed rules and principles for how a state should be governed, sometimes set out in a single document

democracy form of government in which people vote to choose their leaders in elections

European Union collection of countries in Europe that work together for trade and other reasons

government the system and people who are in charge of running a country. In the UK, the government is led by the Prime Minister.

immigrant a person who moves from one country to live permanently in another

judiciary system of judges and law courts who decide how the laws of a country should operate

majority the largest number or part

monarch king or queen

nation community of people who have things in common such as history or language

Parliament the body that makes laws for the United Kingdom, made up of more than 650 Members of Parliament

rights freedoms or protections that citizens can expect to receive, such as the right to free speech

Rule of Law the principle that everyone in a state or country has to follow the law, including the government and police

rural in the countryside or outside a city

tolerance accepting and respecting the right of other people to hold different views or follow a different religion

values principles or ideas that are believed to be important, such as belief in democracy as the best way to govern a country

Further reading and research

Places to visit

There are many places you can visit to discover more about the story of the UK and what it means to be British. Here are just a few of them.

ENGLAND: Chinese New Year, Liverpool: celebrating Britain's diverse community

Houses of Parliament, Westminster: The heart of British democracy

Runnymede on Thames: Where Magna Carta was signed in 1215

Stratford-Upon-Avon: Town devoted to the life and work of William Shakespeare, the greatest writer in English

NORTHERN IRELAND: Giant's Causeway: One of the greatest natural wonders of the UK

SCOTLAND: Scottish Parliament, Edinburgh: Where Scotland's laws have been made since 2004

Skara Brae, Orkney: 5000-year-old village, one of the oldest settlements in the UK

WALES: Pontcysllte Aqueduct: Wonder of British engineering carrying a canal across a river valley

St David's: Religious centre of Wales and the UK's smallest city

Books

Britannia: Great Stories from British History, Geraldine McCaughrean (Orion Children's Books, 2014)

Democracy (Systems of Government), Sean Connolly (Franklin Watts, 2017)

Scotland: A Very Peculiar History, Fiona MacDonald (Book House, 2015)

Young Citizen's Passport, Citizenship Foundation, 16th edition, 2013 – regularly updated guide for young people to British laws, rights and responsibilities

Websites

www.parliament.uk The website of the Houses of Parliament is a great source of information about British democracy.
You can also visit websites for other parliaments and assemblies around the UK:

www.parliament.scot
www.assembly.wales
www.niassembly.gov.uk

www.bbc.co.uk/schools/citizenx/local/democracy/animation.shtml
This animation from the BBC explores school democracy.

www.interfaith.org.uk/youth
The Inter Faith Network promotes mutual respect and understanding between faith communities. Their website includes a section for young people.

Index